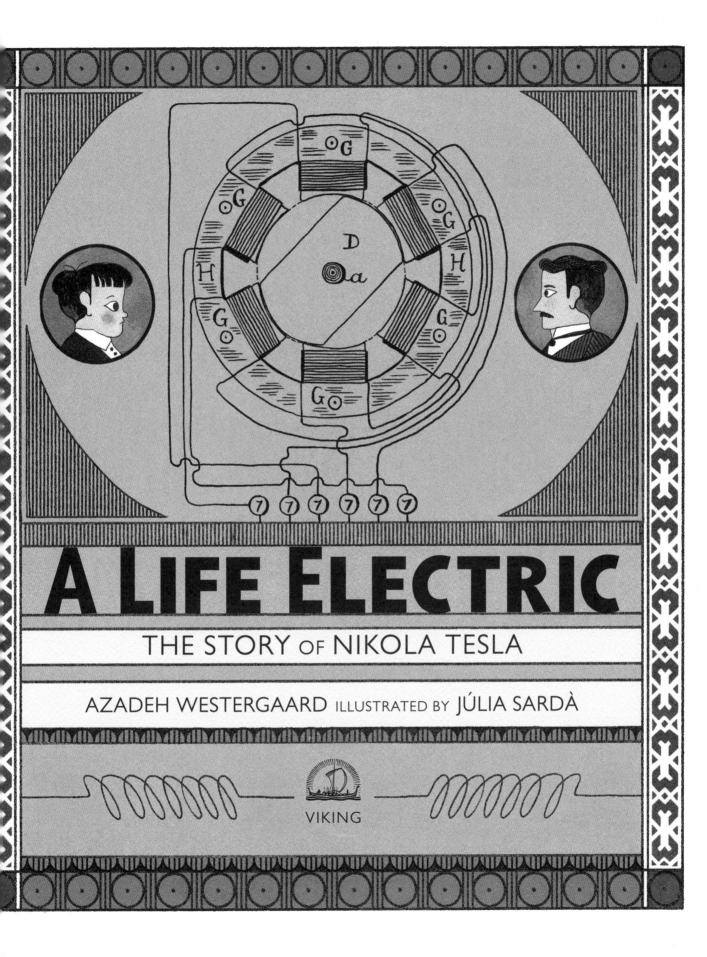

A LIFE ELECTRIC

THE STORY OF NIKOLA TESLA

AZADEH WESTERGAARD ILLUSTRATED BY JÚLIA SARDÀ

VIKING

VIKING

An imprint of Penguin Random House LLC, New York

First published in the United States of America by Viking,
an imprint of Penguin Random House LLC, 2021

Visit us online at penguinrandomhouse.com.

Library of Congress Cataloging-in-Publication Data is available.

Manufactured in China

ISBN 9780593114605

3 5 7 9 10 8 6 4

Design by Opal Roengchai
Text set in Athenaeum Std
This art was created digitally

For my parents, Farideh and Kiyoumars
–A.W.

To Carmela
–J.S.

At the stroke of midnight on July 10, 1856, thunder clapped.

Lightning flashed.

And a baby boy was born.

"He'll be a child of the storm," his nurse said.

"No," his mother replied. "A child of light."

She did not know then that her son, Nikola, would grow up to be both:

one of the most important electrical inventors in the world—

then and now.

Nikola grew up in a farmhouse in a village called Smiljan
at the foot of a wooded hill, next door to a barn
and a small chapel where his father preached.

He loved animals and never missed a day cradling and feeding
his family's chickens, roosters, pigeons, and geese.
He had many playmates, but his best friend was a cat.
The magnificent Mačak.

When Nikola was three,

he stroked his cat and something remarkable happened:

"Mačak's back was a sheet of light and my hand produced a shower of sparks

loud enough to be heard all over the place."

Nikola had never seen anything like it.

His mother said, "Stop playing with the cat, he might start a fire."

His father said, "This is nothing but electricity, the same thing you see on the trees in a storm."

He wondered, *Is Nature a gigantic cat? If so, who strokes its back?*

From that moment on, Nikola could not stop thinking about electricity.

Just like his mother, who sewed clothing by hand
and built new tools to help with housework,
Nikola had a gift for invention.

He dreamt of flying like the pigeons and geese on his farm—
so, he jumped off the roof of his barn holding only an old umbrella.
His bones didn't break, but he was bedbound for weeks.

Before he was six, Nikola had designed:

a metal hook for catching frogs,

a popgun that shattered windows (and got him punished!),

and a rotating motor powered by the fast, flapping wings

of sixteen June bugs.

When he was eight, Nikola fell in love with books.
He remembered everything he read
and soon carried whole volumes in his head.
His father feared he'd go blind and discouraged so much reading—
but Nikola couldn't stop.

While the family slept,
he made his own candles,
stuffed towels in the cracks
of his bedroom door to hide the light,
and worked his way through his
father's library of books.

In school, Nikola got high marks in literature, sciences, and math.
His dream was to study electricity when he grew up,
but his father expected him to follow in his footsteps—
and become a priest.

When he was seventeen, Nikola contracted cholera,
a serious disease that left him barely able to move.
Everyone feared he was at death's door.
Nikola's father promised him he could study anything he wanted—
if only he got better.

Nikola recovered quickly
and soon enrolled in college to pursue his passion—
electrical engineering.

When he was twenty-six,

Nikola and a friend were strolling through a park

and reciting poetry aloud when the solution

to a scientific puzzle came to him like a flash of lightning.

A puzzle he had thought about for years.

A puzzle his university professor had said was impossible to solve.

A detailed image appeared in Nikola's mind,

of a motor sending electric currents along a wire—

forward then backward, forward then backward

like the endless rush and receding sweep of the ocean tide.

Nikola had discovered a new way to transmit electricity over long distances.

And he knew it was an invention that would soon power the world.

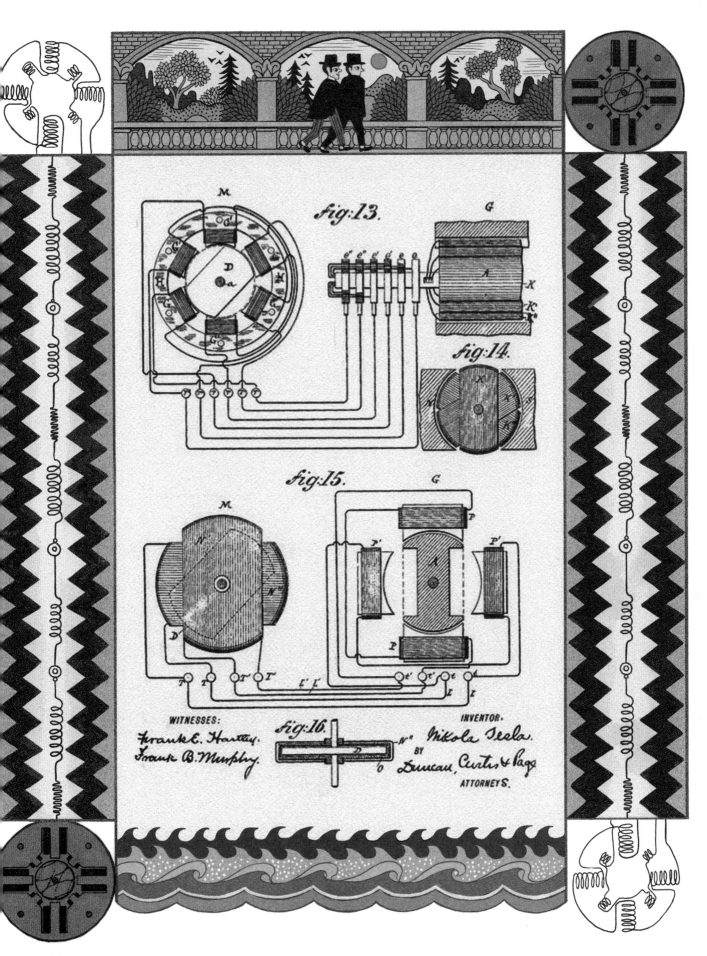

Fig:13.

Fig:14.

Fig:15.

Fig:16.

WITNESSES:
Frank E. Hartley.
Frank B. Murphy.

INVENTOR.
Nikola Tesla.
BY
Duncan, Curtis & Page
ATTORNEYS.

Nikola could think of only one person

who would understand the importance of his idea.

So, he set sail across the Atlantic from Europe to America.

When he arrived in New York, his pockets held:

four pennies,

some handwritten poems,

notes for a flying machine invention,

and a letter of introduction to Thomas Edison,

the inventor of the first practical electric light bulb.

The two men worked together briefly,
but they disagreed about everything—
especially about the future of electricity.

Nikola had no choice but to leave
and find a way to develop
his electric motor on his own.

After years with little success, Nikola partnered with George Westinghouse, a powerful businessman who invited him to present his invention at the 1893 Chicago World's Fair.

Together, the men and their workers toiled day and night building the electric motors that Nikola had once seen so clearly in his mind.

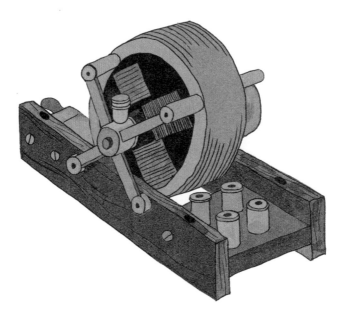

On the fair's opening day, thousands of visitors
from around the world gathered.
The president of the United States pressed a gold telegraph button
that set the fairground's electric machinery in motion.

And for the first time in history,
over a hundred thousand light bulbs lit up at once.

The crowds cheered, trumpets blared, and flags unfurled—
Nikola's *City of Light* had changed the world forever.

N. TESLA

G. WESTINGHOUSE

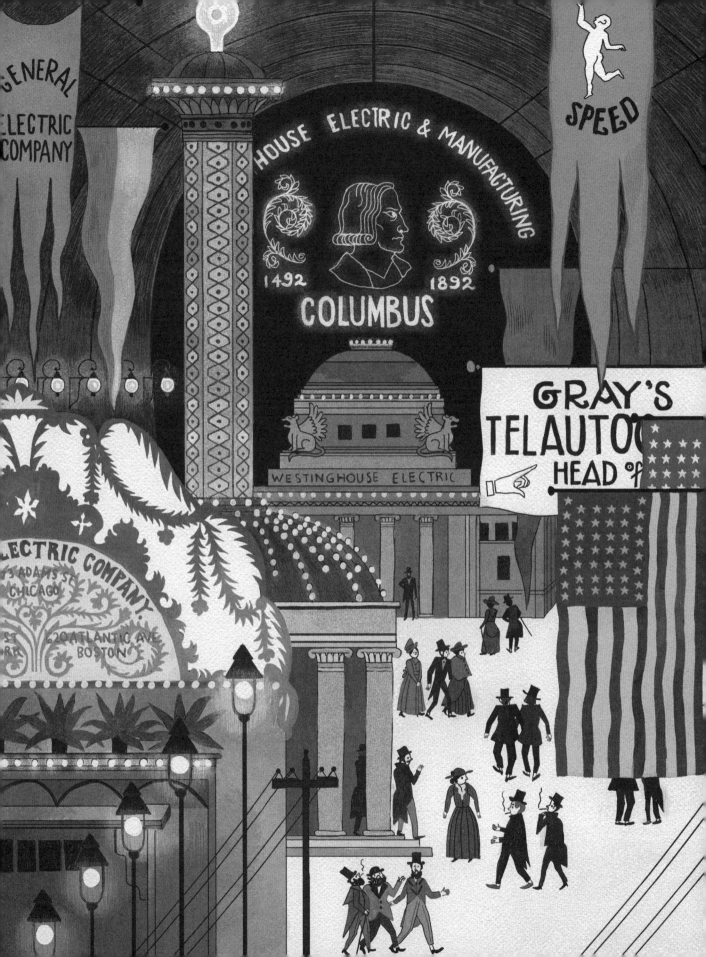

Soon once-darkened homes, office buildings,

and city streets were illuminated.

The wheels of streetcars and electric trains now whirled,

and factories hummed through the night.

Newspaper headlines flashed Nikola's name on every continent.

They called him the *Wizard of Electricity*.

Nikola's invention was a success,

but the businessman who helped him said he was running out of money.

Nikola was trusting—and thankful that this man had believed in his idea.

So, he gave away the rest of the rights to his invention.

And instead of becoming one of the richest men in the world,

Nikola ended up with nothing.

Nikola had a gift for invention, but he was also a creature of habit.

Even as he grew old, he didn't stop memorizing poems by heart,

or solving scientific equations in his head,

or taking long daily walks up and down New York's cobblestoned streets.

He also never stopped loving animals.

Which is why every morning and afternoon,

with a bag filled with birdseed in his pocket,

Nikola stopped by Bryant Park and the steps of St. Patrick's Cathedral

to cradle and feed the city's pigeons.

He never missed a day.

And if he was ever sick or when he got too old to walk,
Nikola hired messenger boys to visit the flocks on his behalf.
"I've been feeding pigeons, thousands of them, for years;
thousands of them, for who can tell," he said.

Nikola always looked for ill or injured pigeons,
to either nurse at home or hand-deliver to the local animal hospital.
Before making a diagnosis, he would peer into each bird's eyes,
then inspect their wings, beaks, and feet.
"Caring for homeless, hungry, or sick birds is the delight of my life," he said.

Nikola's New York home was almost always a humble hotel room,
where his windows were open for pigeons to come and go,
where neat rows of nesting baskets lined his bedroom bureaus,
where bowls filled with fresh water and seeds lay waiting on his sill.

As the years went on, people began taking Nikola's inventions for granted.
No one recognized the *Wizard of Electricity* on the city streets anymore.
Now newspapers flashed headlines about an unusual old man,
scattering seeds in the park.
They called him the *Pigeon Charmer of New York,*
and when reporters asked about his devotion to birds, he simply said:
"All things from childhood are still dear to me."

When the old man died in his hotel room, penniless and alone,
with the windows wide open and birdseed on his sill,
the mayor of New York announced the sad news on the radio:
"He was a feather in the cap of the whole human race."

Nikola was gone, but now he was remembered—
as thousands of mourners from around the world
flocked to attend the funeral in honor of his life.

His name was Nikola Tesla.

A gifted inventor, a creature of habit.

A lover of animals, a friend to humankind.

A child of the storm, a child of the light.

A human flash of lightning, far ahead of his time.

AUTHOR'S NOTE

NIKOLA TESLA was born on July 10, 1856, to Serbian parents in Smiljan, a mountain village in what is now modern-day Croatia. A prolific inventor, his patents encompassed radar, X-ray, and remote-control technology; wireless radio communications—Tesla, and not Guglielmo Marconi (1874–1937), is considered the father of radio, thanks to a 1943 Supreme Court ruling upholding Tesla's patent precedence over Marconi's; the Tesla coil (a device that can discharge bolts of lightning by transforming low alternating current into extremely high voltages through the release of a spark); and most importantly, the AC (alternating current) induction motor, which uses alter-

Nikola Tesla, ca. 1890.
Courtesy of Special Collections, Fine Arts Library, Harvard University.

nating currents to efficiently distribute electricity along far distances and which continues to be the world's standard form of electric distribution.

How to power an electric motor using alternating currents had tormented Tesla for years. He was twenty-six years old and strolling in a park with a friend when the setting sun inspired him to recite the following passage from Goethe's *Faust* from memory:

> *The glow retreats, done is the day of toil;*
> *It yonder hastes, new fields of life exploring;*
> *Ah, that no wing can lift me from the soil,*
> *Upon its track to follow, follow soaring!*

And like a flash of lightning, a clear image of a working AC induction motor formed in his mind. Tesla wrote of the experience: "I cannot begin to describe my emotions. Pygmalion seeing his statue come to life could not have been more deeply moved. A thousand secrets of nature which I might have stumbled upon accidentally, I would have given for that one which I had wrestled from her against all odds, and at the peril of my existence."

Tesla moved to America to work with Thomas Edison (1847–1931), the famous inventor who introduced the world to the phonograph (the precursor to the record player) and the first commercially viable incandescent electric light bulb. Among his countless innovations, Edison also developed a pioneering electrical grid system that used direct-current (DC) electricity to illuminate previously candlelit and gas-flamed homes and streets. Yet Edison's electrical system, while revolutionary, also had significant drawbacks. Direct-current electrical energy, which traveled in only one direction, dissipated and weakened as it ran through the wires, limiting how far it could travel. Thus, in order to meet the electrical needs of a city like New York, power stations would need to be built every square mile.

Tesla believed his AC induction motor was the solution to the limitations of Edison's direct current–powered system. With Tesla's invention, alternating currents did not lose energy as they traveled through the wires, and high-voltage electricity flowing through a single power station could easily be transformed into lower currents to safely meet the needs of homes and buildings for miles. However, Edison dismissed Tesla's AC-powered system as impractical and inherently dangerous, which soon led to the end of their working relationship.

When the wealthy businessman and inventor George Westinghouse (1846–1914) began developing his own AC-powered system in direct competition with Edison's DC-powered system, a contentious professional feud began, which the press coined the *War of Currents*. Edison was a shrewd businessman and knew that only one electrical distribution system could prevail in lighting the world. As such, he initiated an aggressive propaganda campaign to sway public opinion on the inherent dangers of AC electricity by publicly electrocuting dogs, cats, and even an elephant using high-voltage alternating currents.

When Tesla patented his AC-powered induction motor and related technology, Westing-house immediately purchased his invention for tens of thousands of dollars. The men's business agreement also included a generous royalty payment of $2.50 for every unit of horsepower generated by Tesla's motors. However, when Westinghouse's company later ran into financial troubles, Tesla, in a gesture of goodwill, tore up their business contract and agreed to forgo any future royalties. Had Tesla held on to his royalty agreement, or at the very least negotiated a lower rate, he would have become extremely wealthy and would have had all the money he needed to continue his scientific work without any financial burdens.

Westinghouse and Edison's feud came to a close when, with Tesla's patents in hand, Westinghouse's company won the contract to power the 1893 World's Columbian Exposition (also known as the Chicago World's Fair), which commemorated the four-hundred-year anniversary of Columbus's arrival in the Americas. An estimated 300,000 visitors witnessed the historic opening ceremony on May 1, when Grover Cleveland (1837–1908), then president of the United States, pushed a telegraph button that powered the fair's enormous machinery and lit up the fairgrounds with over 100,000 lightbulbs all at once. As the orchestra played "My Country 'Tis of Thee," the awestruck crowd cheered, waved handkerchiefs, and sang along.

1893 Columbia Exposition.
© George Westinghouse Museum Collection,
Detre Library & Archives, Heinz History Center.

In fact, the illuminated fairground was so enchanting that it inspired the writer L. Frank Baum's Emerald City of Oz. In total, over twenty-eight million visitors from around the world visited the fair, which also introduced the public to the first mechanical dishwasher, the Ferris wheel, and the zipper, to name just a few innovations. Westinghouse and Tesla's hard work paid off—Westinghouse Electric's AC-powered electrical distribution system at the fair was an enormous success and marked the beginning of an entirely new way of life for the world.

Despite Tesla's sudden fame and fortune, the immense significance of his contributions to modern life fell through the cracks of public knowledge in the last decades of his own life. Newspaper articles now focused on his eccentric habits and money troubles, or included tongue-in-cheek editorials related to his passion for pigeons. Much like his childhood cat, the magnificent Măcak, one particular animal stood out as the singular object of his affection in his later years—a white pigeon with brown-tipped wings: "No matter where I was that pigeon would find me; when I wanted her, I had only to wish and call her and she would come flying to me."

Tesla's friends always commented on his deeply loving nature, sensitive soul, and pro-found affinity and respect for all living beings. In Tesla's own words, he had an "instinctive impulse" throughout his life "to harness the energies of nature to the service of man." As he wrote in "A Story of Youth Told by Age," the letter he sent to his friend's young daughter, Pola Fotitch: "I often visualize the events of my youth to find relief from great and dangerous mental strain." By connecting with pigeons, which not only were living symbols of Tesla's hap-piest childhood memories but also are considered to be

White bird.
© Nikola Tesla Museum/Photo Library.

nature's original wireless messengers, Tesla was able to bridge the gulf between his past and present.

Nikola Tesla died alone and penniless in Room 3327 on the thirty-third floor of the Hotel New Yorker on January 7, 1943, yet over two thousand science, business, and arts luminaries from around the world attended his funeral at New York's Cathedral of St. John the Divine. In a radio broadcast announcing his death, the mayor of New York, Fiorello La Guardia, read a tribute written by Tesla's friend, the author Louis Adamic, in which he quoted the engineer B.A. Behrend: "Were we to eliminate from our industrial world the results of Tesla's work, the wheels of industry would cease to turn, and our electric trains and cars would stop, our towns would be dark, our mills and fac-tories dead and idle. So far reaching is his work . . . should Tesla's work be suddenly withdrawn—darkness would prevail."

Nikola Tesla with Tesla coil.
© George Westinghouse Museum
Collection, Detre Library & Archives, Heinz History Center.

SOURCES

Books and Letters

Carlson, W. Bernard. *Tesla: Inventor of the Electrical Age*. Princeton, NJ: Princeton University Press, 2013.

Cheney, Margaret. *Tesla, Man Out of Time*. Englewood Cliffs, NJ: Prentice Hall, 1981.

Jonnes, Jill. *Empires of Light: Edison, Tesla, Westinghouse, and the Race to Electrify the World*. New York: Random House, 2003.

O'Neill, John J. *Prodigal Genius: The Life of Nikola Tesla*. Kempton, IL: Adventures Unlimited Press, 2008.

Seifer, Marc J. *Wizard: The Life and Times of Nikola Tesla: Biography of a Genius*. New York: Citadel Press, 1998.

Tesla, Nikola. *My Inventions: An Autobiography*. Edited by David Major. Australia: Philovox, 2013.

Tesla, Nikola. "A Story of Youth Told by Age." PBS. pbs.org/tesla/ll/story_youth.html.

Film, Radio, and Websites

EXPO: Magic of the White City. Directed by Mark Bussler. Inecom Entertainment Company, 2005.

"La Guardia Tribute to Nikola Tesla." The NYPR Archive Collections, WNYC Archives ID: 2977. wnyc.org/story/la-guardia-tribute-to-nicola-tesla.

Tesla: Master of Lightning. Directed by Robert Uth. New Voyage Communications, 2000.

Tesla. Written and produced by David Grubin. American Experience, 2016.

"Opening Day." The World's Fair Chicago 1893. worldsfairchicago1893.com/home/fair/history/opening-day. Accessed on April 18, 2020.

The Pigeoneers. Directed by Alessandro Croseri. Alessandro Croseri Productions, 2008.

Newspaper Articles

"At Night and in Secret Nikola Tesla Lavishes Money and Love on Pigeons." *New York World*, November 21, 1926.

"Dr. Tesla Gives Home to an Errant Pigeon That Flew Into 40th-Story Room in Hotel." *The New York Times*, February 6, 1935.

"Nikola Tesla Dies; Prolific Inventor." *The New York Times*, January 8, 1943.

"Nursing Sick Birds Is Inventor's Hobby." *The New York Times*, April 15, 1927.

"Opened by the President." *The New York Times*, May 2, 1893.

"Park Pigeons Fed, Inventor Pays Bill." *Democrat and Chronicle*, May 1, 1937.

"Tesla Is Provider of Pigeon Relief." *The New York Times*, May 1, 1937.

Quotes

"He'll be a child of the storm . . ." Carlson, W. Bernard. *Tesla: Inventor of the Electrical Age*. Princeton, NJ: Princeton University Press, 2013, p. 18.

"Mačak's back was a sheet of light . . ." Tesla, Nikola. "A Story of Youth Told by Age." PBS. pbs.org/tesla/ll/story_youth.html.

"I've been feeding pigeons . . ." O'Neill, John J. *Prodigal Genius: The Life of Nikola Tesla*. Kempton, IL: Adventures Unlimited Press, 2008, p. 316.

"Caring for homeless . . ." "At Night and in Secret Nikola Tesla Lavishes Money and Love on Pigeons," *New York World*, November 21, 1926, p. 1.

"All things from childhood . . ." Cheney, Margaret. *Tesla, Man Out of Time*. Englewood Cliffs, NJ: Prentice Hall, 1981, p. 271.

"He was a feather in the cap . . ." "La Guardia Tribute to Nikola Tesla." The NYPR Archive Collections, WNYC Archives ID: 2977. wnyc.org/story/la-guardia-tribute-to-nicola-tesla.

"He was twenty-six years old . . ." Tesla, Nikola. *My Inventions: An Autobiography*. Edited by David Major. Australia: Philovox, 2013, p. 35.

"I cannot begin to describe . . ." Tesla. *My Inventions*, p. 35.

"No matter where I was . . ." O'Neill. *Prodigal Genius*, p. 316.

"Instinctive impulse . . ." Tesla. *My Inventions*, p. 22.

"I often visualize the events of my youth . . ." Tesla. "A Story of Youth Told by Age."

"Were we to eliminate . . ." "La Guardia Tribute to Nikola Tesla."